THE GREAT BARRIER REEF BOOK

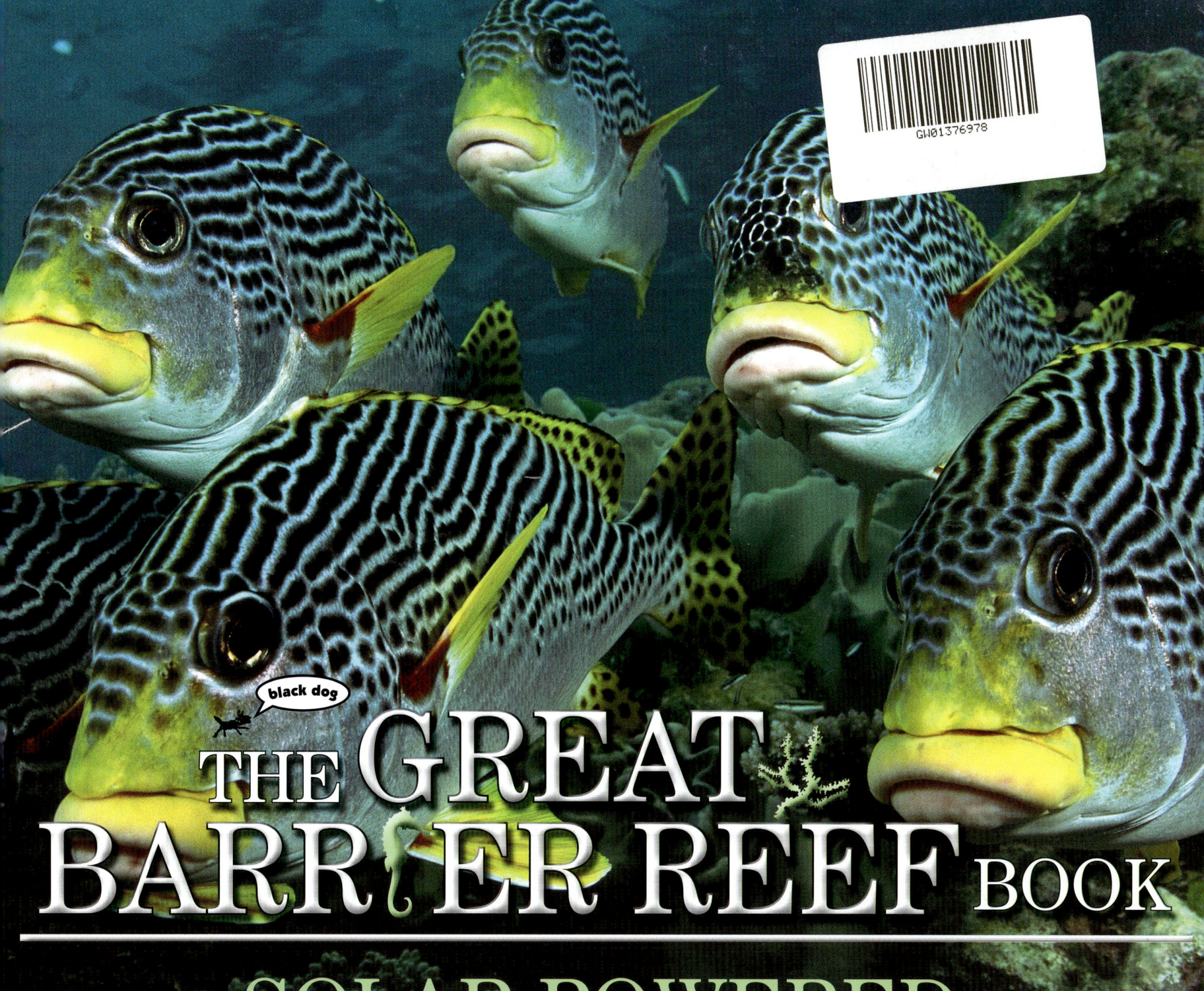

black dog

SOLAR POWERED

by Dr Mark Norman

Dr Mark Norman is a research scientist at Museum Victoria. He did his PhD on the octopuses of the Great Barrier Reef.

First published in 2009 by
black dog books
15 Gertrude Street
Fitzroy Vic 3065
Australia
61 + 3 + 9419 9406
61 + 3 + 9419 1214 (fax)
www.bdb.com.au
dog@bdb.com.au

Dr Mark Norman asserts the moral right to be identified as the author of this Work.

Copyright text © Mark Norman 2009
Copyright layout and design © black dog books

All rights reserved. Apart from any fair dealing for the purpose of study, research, criticism or review, as permitted under the Copyright Act, no part of this book may be reproduced by any process, stored in a retrieval system, or transmitted in any form, without permission of the copyright owner. All enquiries should be made to the publisher at the address above.

Designed by Blue Boat Design
Printed and bound in China by Everbest Printing International

Mixed Sources
Product group from well-managed forests, and other controlled sources
www.fsc.org Cert no. SGS-COC-003563
© 1996 Forest Stewardship Council

FSC is a non-profit international organisation established to promote the responsible management of the world's forests.

National Library of Australia
cataloguing-in-publication data:
Norman, Mark (Mark Douglas)
The Great Barrier Reef Book: Solar Powered.

Bibliography
Includes Index
For primary school children.
ISBN: 9781742030319 (pbk)

Subjects: Solar energy—Queensland—Great Barrier Reef
Juvenile literature

Dewey Number: 919.43

10 9 8 7 6 5 4 3 2   10 11 12 13

Photo credits:
Gary Bell / oceanwideimages: pp 2-3, 4-5, 6-7, 9, 10-11, 12, 16, 17, 19, 20-21, 25, 26-27, 29; istock: pp 20, back cover, front cover; Joanna Browne: p 4; shutterstock: pp ii, iii, 4, 13, 28-29; Norbert Wu / Minden Pictures / National Geographic: pp i, 18-19; Mark Norman: pp 3, 4, 5, 6, 8-9, 13, 22, 30; Photodisk: p25; Roger Steene: pp 9, 12-13, 14-15; Nasa Images: p 6; Scott R. Santos: p 8, BigStock: p 23

CONTENTS

FORESTS OF STONE	2
ALL RUN ON SUNLIGHT	3
A MILLION COLOURS	4
WHERE IN THE WORLD?	6
PLANT POWER Zooxanthellae	8
SNEAKY SLUGS Nudibranch	9
A FISH CARWASH Cleaner Shrimp	10
SPINED AND DANGEROUS Lionfish	11
CLOWNS IN SLIME Clownfish	12
A SNOT SLEEPING BAG Parrotfish	14
A SWIMMING SNAKE Olive Sea Snake	16
NIGHT HUNTER Blue Ribbon Eel	17
FRIENDLY BIG SPOTS Potato Cod	18
OCEAN VOYAGERS Green Turtle	20
A SOLAR-POWERED SHELL Giant Clam	22
ANCIENT GIANTS Brain Coral	23
FLYING GIANTS Manta Ray	24
TREES OF STONE Staghorn Coral	26
CLIMATE CHANGE: WHAT WE CAN DO	28
GLOSSARY AND INDEX	30

FORESTS OF STONE

The Great Barrier Reef is like a gigantic underwater forest. It is over 2000 kilometres long and every corner is teeming with colourful animals. Everything is alive or made by living creatures.

Coral is made up of millions of tiny star-shaped animals known as **polyps** (poll-ips). All the polyps in one coral **colony** work together to make the hard parts of the coral. Different types of corals grow in different ways to make wonderful shapes and sizes.

The Great Barrier Reef has formed over millions of years in the shallow warm waters off north-eastern Australia. It's a perfect place to soak up the sun.

ALL RUN ON SUNLIGHT

Amazingly, the whole Great Barrier Reef is run on **solar** power. The corals that build the Great Barrier Reef and many of the animals that live there make their food from sunlight. The corals farm tiny plants that live within the coral's body, and in return the plants change sunlight into food for the coral.

Climate change is not good for the Great Barrier Reef. There are thousands of things we can do to fight climate change and keep the Great Barrier Reef safe and healthy. See the back of this book for things you can do right now.

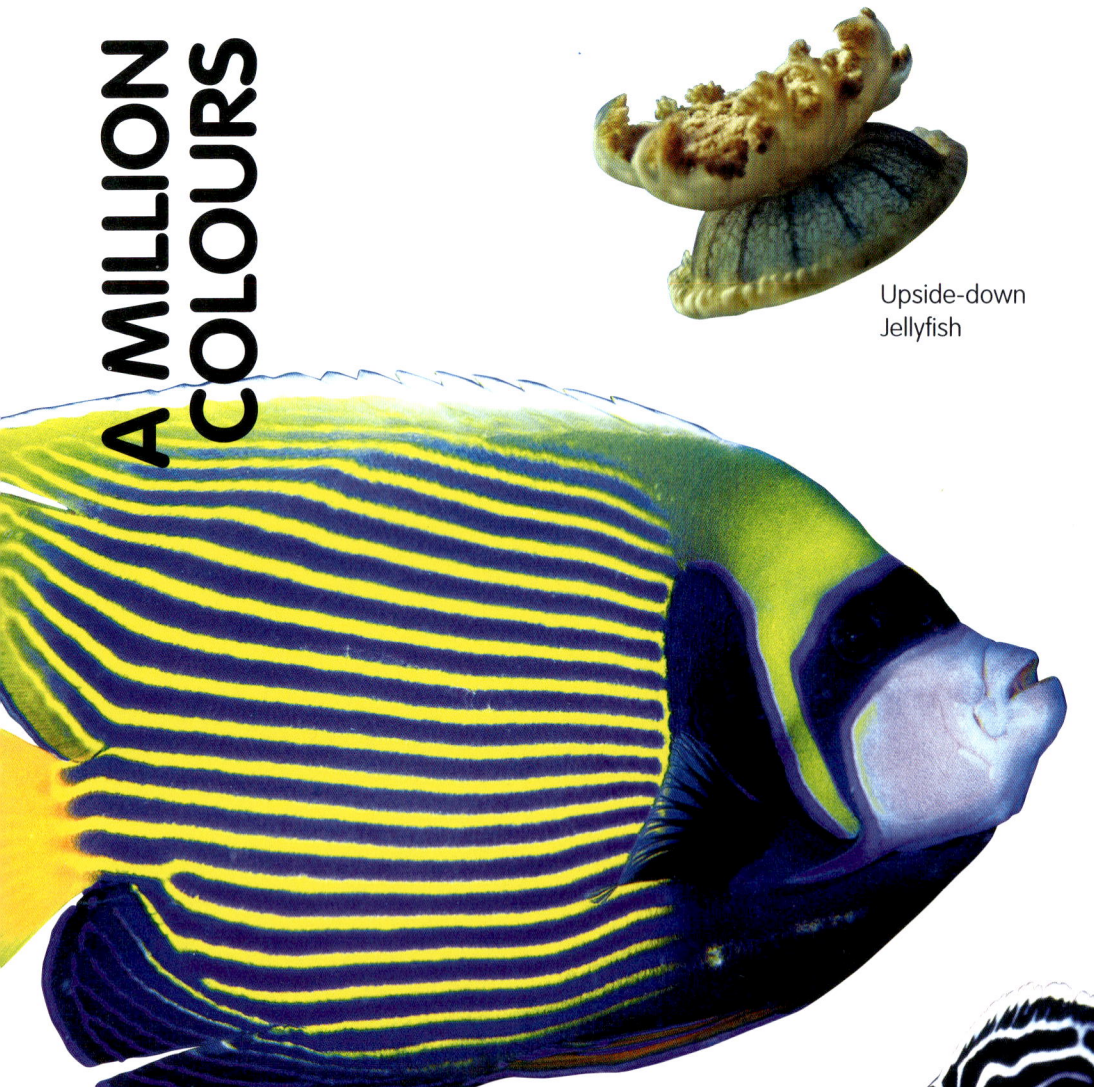

A MILLION COLOURS

Upside-down Jellyfish

Ring-tailed Maori Wrasse

The Great Barrier Reef is home to thousands of creatures, some of which are found nowhere else on earth.

Emperor Angelfish

Emperor Angelfish make a loud, low thumping noise by grinding together parts of their mouth.

Young angelfish look very different from adults.

Young Angelfish

Blackside Hawkfish

Saddled Butterflyfish

Many butterflyfish have long, thin mouths that they use to reach hard-to-get bits of living coral or little crabs and shrimp.

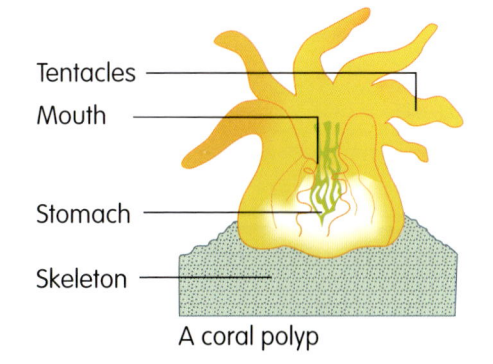

Tentacles
Mouth
Stomach
Skeleton

A coral polyp

Fan coral with little polyps

The coral on the Great Barrier Reef is made by millions of tiny animals called polyps. A polyp is shaped like a bag with a ring of tentacles on the top and a mouth in the middle. Polyps divide in half to make identical copies of themselves—this is how coral grows. In many corals, the polyps lay down a cement layer underneath them that join together to make the hard coral branches.

Glass Shrimp on **anemone** tentacles

Spotted Angelfish

WHERE IN THE WORLD?

Quick facts:

Where is it?
Off the north-east corner of Australia.

How many reefs?
About 3650 individual reefs.

How big is it?
Around 2000 kilometres long, with a total area of around 350 000 square kilometres.

How old is it?
It is 6000 to 9000 years old, but has probably existed on and off in this area for 25 million years.

How warm is the water?
Mostly 22-31°C, but the water can get as hot as 36°C in the small lagoons.

Who lives there?
There are 3500 fish **species**, 390 coral species and tens of thousands of **invertebrate** species.

The Great Barrier Reef is so huge that it is the only structure made by living creatures that can be seen from space!

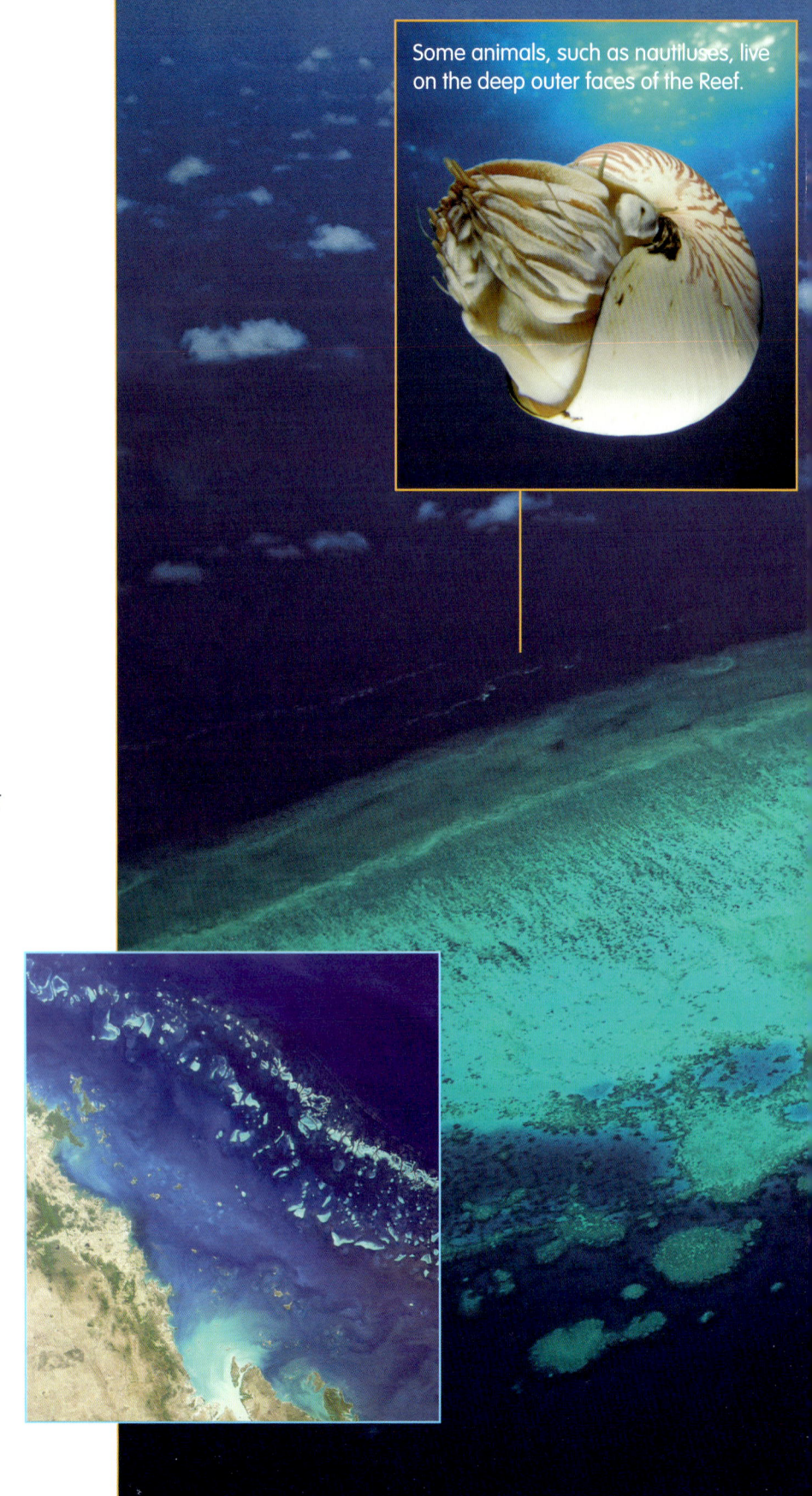

Some animals, such as nautiluses, live on the deep outer faces of the Reef.

Reef face: the strongest corals hold back the force of the ocean waves.

Coral atoll: **Atolls** are rings of reefs or islands.

Lagoon: Calm lagoons form inside rings of reef.

Channel: a gap between reefs.

Cay: Coral cays are piles of coral rubble or sand washed up by storms.

Islands form as cays get tall enough to support plant life.

Size: 0.01 mm

Food: sunlight

Predators: sea slugs

0.01 mm

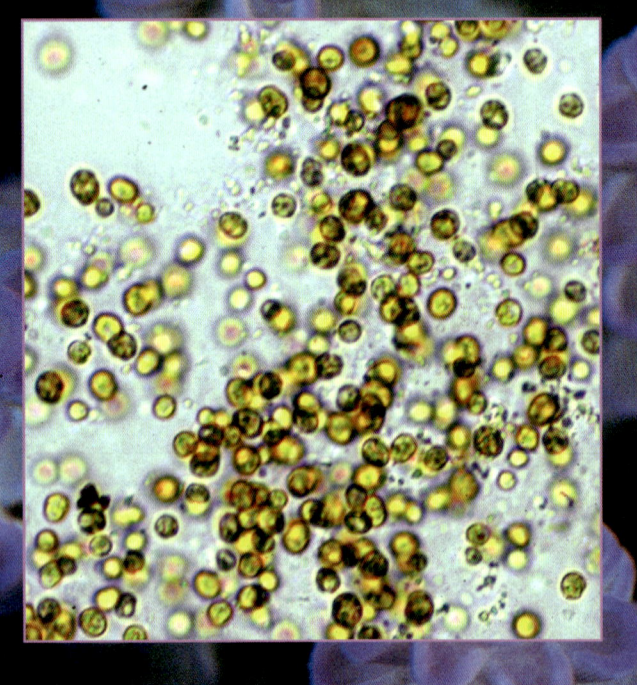

These tiny plant cells are the power supply for the entire Great Barrier Reef. They are so small you could fit 100 across the head of a pin!

Billions of tiny zooxanthellae (pronounced zoo-o-zan-thel-lay) plants live inside the bodies of corals, where they are protected by the coral's stinging tentacles. In return for their cosy homes, they take sunlight and turn it into food, just like plants do on land.

The more sun they get, the more sugars they make. It's the sugars that feed the corals, make them grow and let them build giant reefs of hard skeletons.

PLANT POWER
ZOOXANTHELLAE
(Symbiodinium kawagutii)

SNEAKY SLUGS
NUDIBRANCH
(*Phyllodesmium longicirrum*)

Size: 120 mm

Food: sunlight and soft corals

Predators: other sea slugs

Even sea slugs use solar power, but they do it by stealing the bits they need. This slug has a special stomach with lots of frilly branches. The slug eats corals, filling its stomach with the zooxanthellae plant cells. It can even use the poisons from the coral it eats to protect itself! This way it can glide around eating coral, using sunlight to make its own sugars, and is safe with its poisonous skin.

Other kinds of sea slugs eat poisonous sponges and use bright colours to show that they're deadly to eat.

10

Size:	60 mm
Food:	parasites, things stuck in the teeth and scales of big fishes.
Predators:	naughty fish!

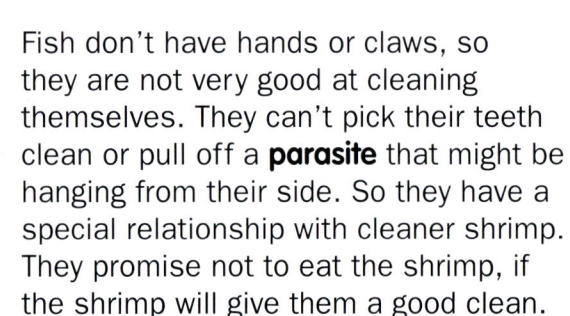

A FISH CARWASH
CLEANER SHRIMP
(Lysmata amboinensis)

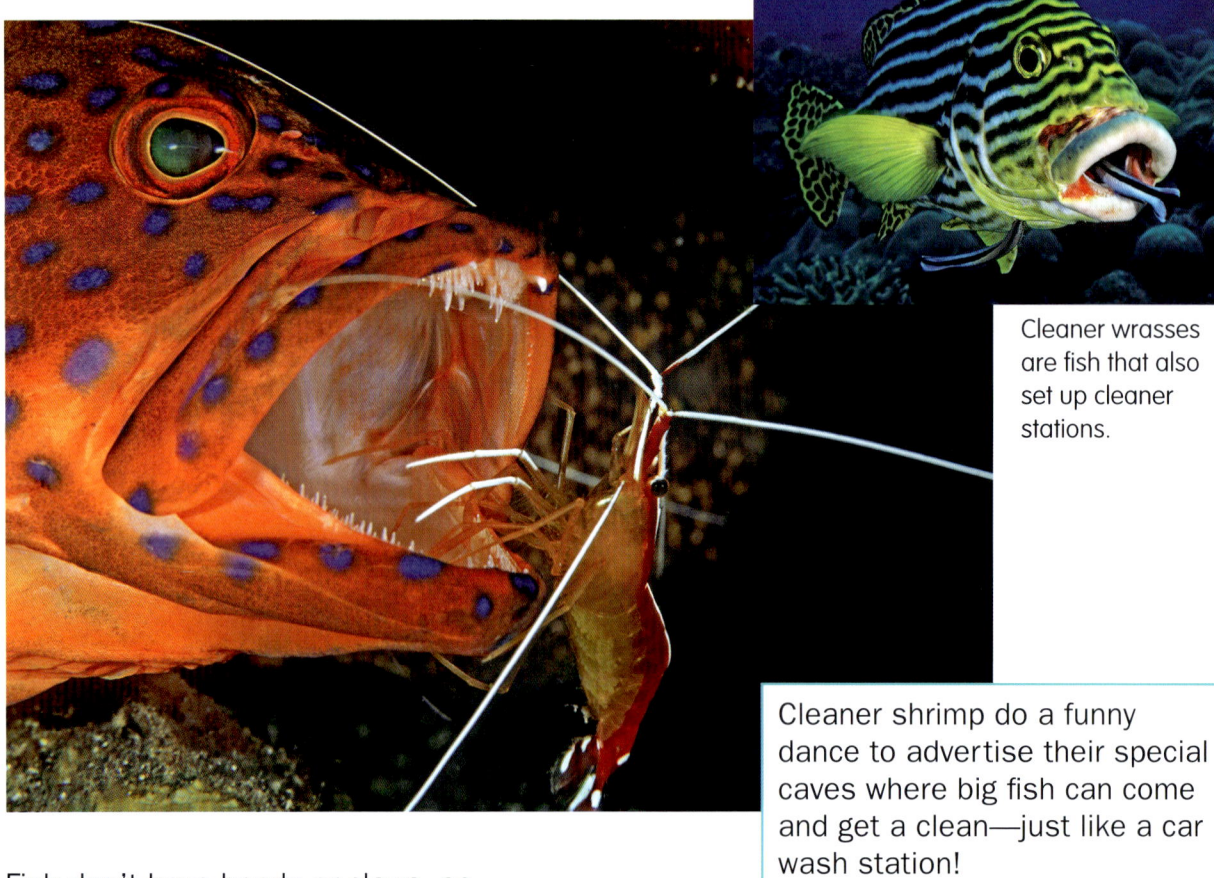

Cleaner wrasses are fish that also set up cleaner stations.

Cleaner shrimp do a funny dance to advertise their special caves where big fish can come and get a clean—just like a car wash station!

Fish don't have hands or claws, so they are not very good at cleaning themselves. They can't pick their teeth clean or pull off a **parasite** that might be hanging from their side. So they have a special relationship with cleaner shrimp. They promise not to eat the shrimp, if the shrimp will give them a good clean.

SPINED AND DANGEROUS
LIONFISH
(Pterois volitans)

The bright, banded patterns on lionfish tell bigger fish that they are armed and dangerous.

Lionfish get their name from the spines around their body, which look like the mane of a lion. The spines have poisonous tips that protect the lionfish from being attacked. Lionfish herd smaller fish into a corner, and spread their spines to stop them escaping. Then they lean in close and shoot out their mouth to suck in the fish.

Size: 350 mm

Food: small fish

Predators: none known US!!!

CLOWNS IN SLIME
CLOWNFISH
(Amphiprion percula)

Lots of creatures cooperate with each other for food and protection. This is called **symbiosis** (sim-by-o-sis).

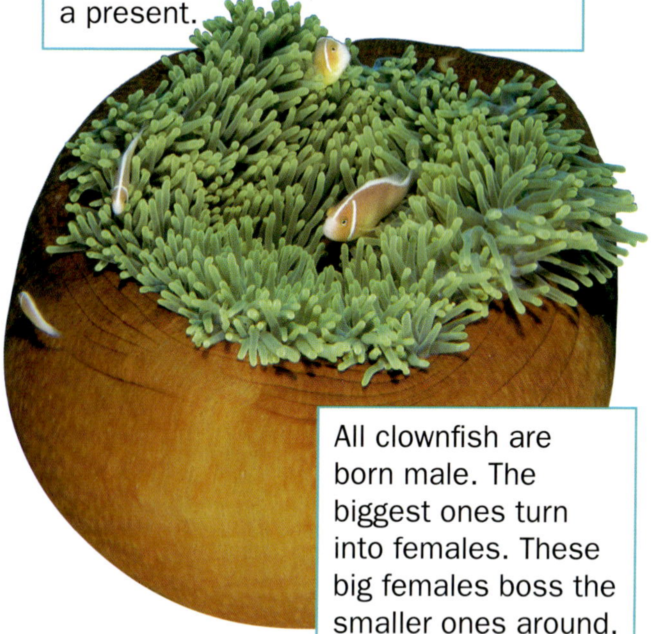

Clownfish live amongst the stinging tentacles of large frilly animals known as anemones. Anemones are shaped like a big beanbag with fat tentacles on top.

If a normal fish swims into the tentacles, it would be stung, paralysed and eaten by the anemone. But a clownfish stays safe by having a special coat of slime, which is just like the anemone's own slime. When the clownfish touches a tentacle, the anemone doesn't feel anything different from its own tentacles, so doesn't shoot off its deadly stinging cells.

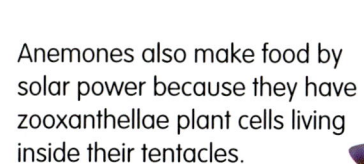

Anemones also make food by solar power because they have zooxanthellae plant cells living inside their tentacles.

Clownfish feed on small animals and scraps of food that float by. Clownfish have small mouths, so if they find something too big to eat they will bring it over and drop it into the anemone's waiting tentacles as a present.

All clownfish are born male. The biggest ones turn into females. These big females boss the smaller ones around, and this stops them changing from male to female.

Size: 110 mm

Food: plankton, food scraps

Predators: large fish

A SNOT SLEEPING BAG
PARROTFISH
(Chlorurus bleekeri)

Imagine if your bedtime involved blowing a giant bubble of snot and climbing inside to sleep. That's normal for parrotfish. They make this slimy sleeping sack every night to hide their fishy smell so that night hunters like eels can't track them down.

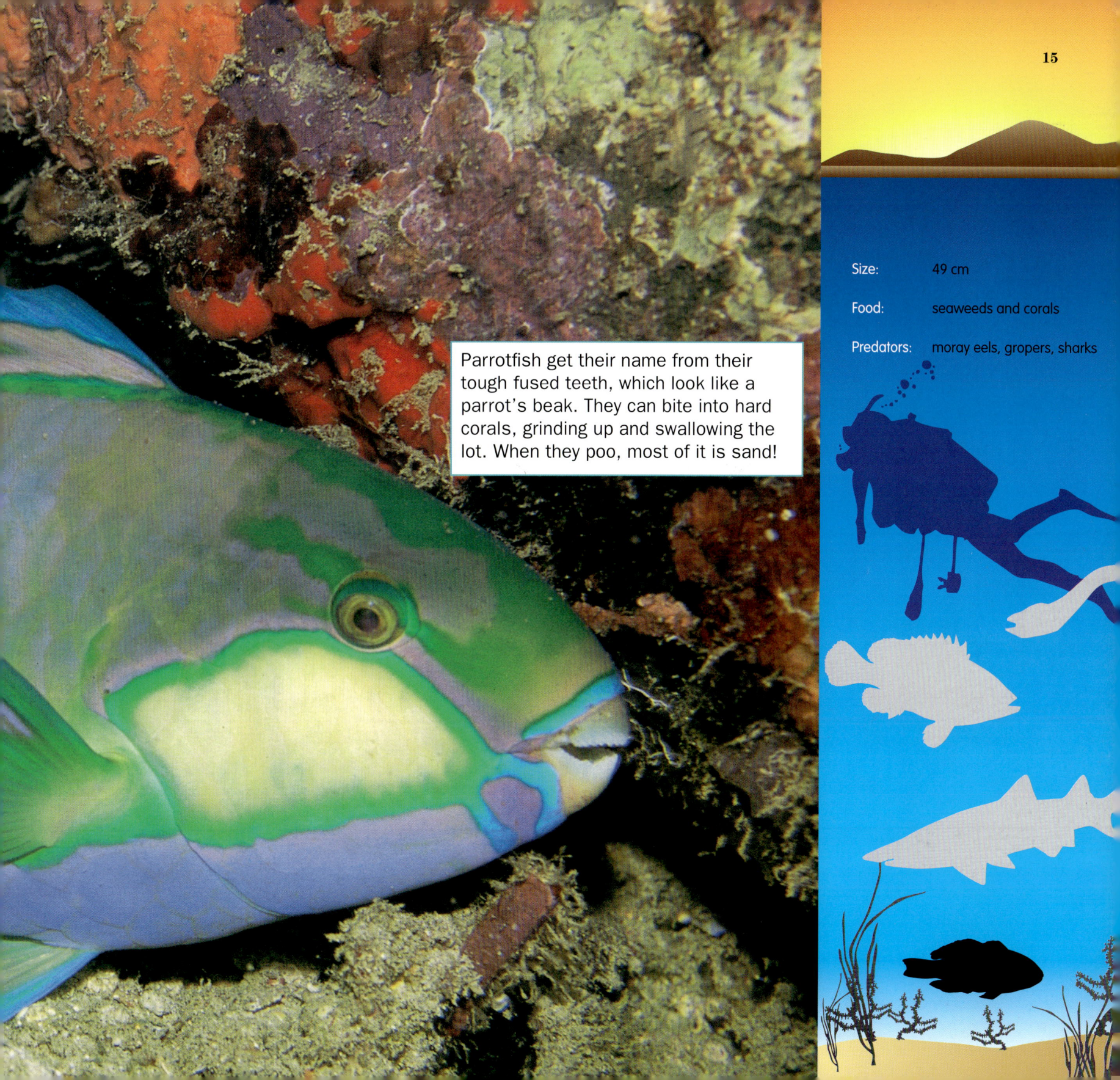

Parrotfish get their name from their tough fused teeth, which look like a parrot's beak. They can bite into hard corals, grinding up and swallowing the lot. When they poo, most of it is sand!

Size: 49 cm

Food: seaweeds and corals

Predators: moray eels, gropers, sharks

16

Size: 1.7 m

Food: small fish

Predators: sharks

Sea snakes spend their whole lives at sea, using their flattened tail to swim. These snakes breathe air, so when they hunt they need to take a big breath from above the water. Some can dive as far as 100 metres deep and back on a single breath.

Sea snakes hunt by trapping fish in caves or burrows. They smell using their forked tongue, licking the water to check for the smell of fish. They have deadly venom but small fangs, so rarely bite divers.

Sea snakes are curious, and will tangle around divers' legs and lick their wetsuits.

A SWIMMING SNAKE
OLIVE SEA SNAKE

(Aipysurus laevis)

NIGHT HUNTER
BLUE RIBBON EEL
(Rhinomuraena quaesita)

This colourful eel lives deep in a burrow, usually sticking only its head out. If a **predator** comes along, it quickly disappears down the hole. It comes out to hunt in the half-light of dusk and dawn, and smells for fish using its large flared nostrils. It uses its razor-sharp teeth to grip fish.

All blue ribbon eels are born male and some turn into females when they get big. Only females are blue.

Sometimes two eels will share the same hole.

Size: 1.3 m

Food: fish

Predators: gropers, sharks

FRIENDLY BIG SPOTS
POTATO COD
(Epinephalus tukula)

Because potato cod are so friendly it was once easy for divers to hunt them. These fish are now fully protected by the law.

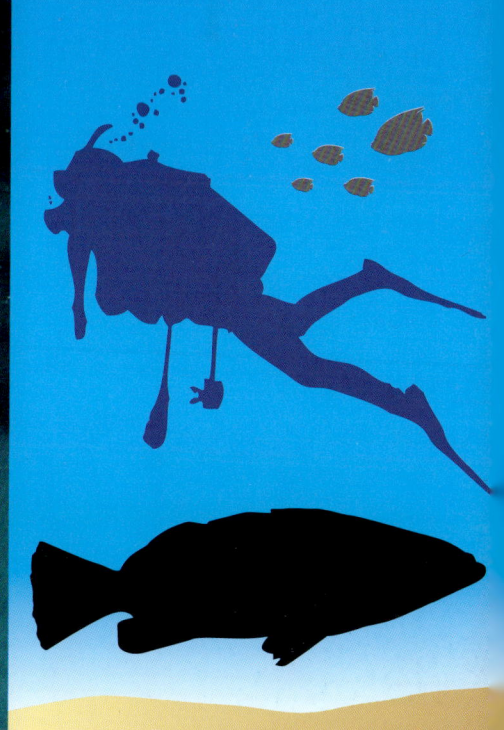

Divers have to resist cuddling potato cod, as they can accidentally scrape off the protective layer of slime that stops the fish getting skin ulcers.

This is one of the friendliest fish on the Great Barrier Reef. It is very curious and will come close to divers to say hello. It feeds by suction, moving close to a fish then quickly opening its big mouth, sucking in lots of water and the fish along with it.

Size:	2 m
Food:	fish
Predators:	sharks

OCEAN VOYAGERS
GREEN TURTLE
(Chelonia mydas)

Whether baby turtles are boys or girls depends on the temperature of the sand the eggs are buried in. Hotter sand causes the young turtles to be girls, while cooler sand makes boy turtles.

Green turtles are great ocean swimmers. They can swim more than 4000 kilometres in their lifetime, which can be over 80 years.

Size:	shell to 1 m long
Food:	seagrass, seaweeds, jellyfish, sponges
Predators:	tiger sharks

Green turtles have a sharp round beak that can chomp up seagrass and seaweed. They also eat jellyfish, and their tough tongue ensures they can't be hurt by the jellyfish's stinging tentacles. Turtles sleep underwater—they take a big breath, stick their head in a cave and sleep for two to three hours.

To lay their eggs, female turtles swim up on the beaches of coral islands at night and dig a deep hole in the sand. They lay around 100 soft leathery eggs into the hole and bury them with sand. Two months later the baby turtles crawl out at night and scamper into the sea.

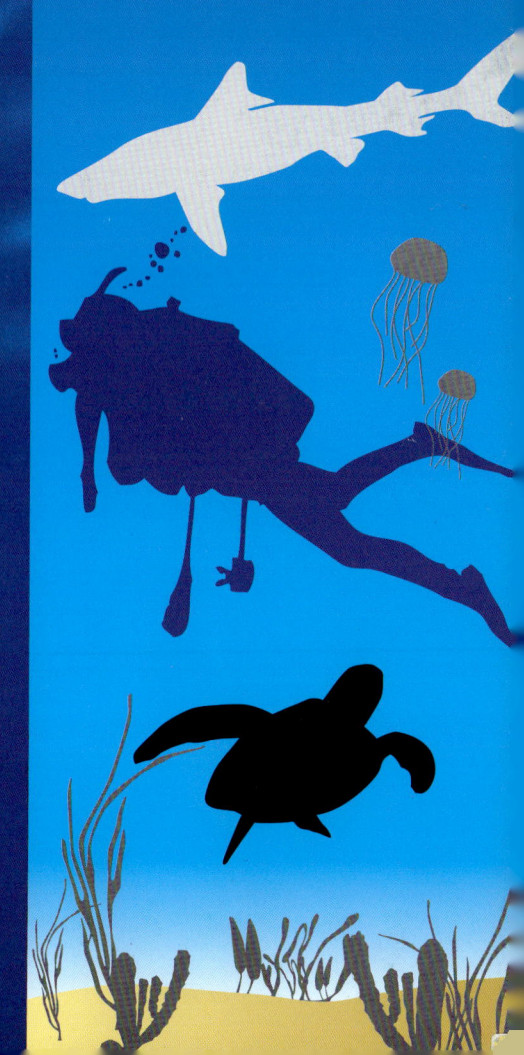

Size:	over 1.4 m
Food:	sunlight, some plankton
Predators:	young clams taken by octopuses and sharks

A SOLAR-POWERED SHELL
GIANT CLAM
(Tridacna gigas)

Giant clams live a long time—at least 50 years, and sometimes up to 100 years!

Giant clams can weigh up to 250 kg—that's about the same as eight children! Some people used to think that these big clams could catch your foot and drown you, but that only happens in the movies. When the shell is open the clam's beautifully coloured skin spreads out in the sunlight. This is because it contains the same solar-powered tiny zooxanthellae plants as the corals. So the biggest shell in the world also runs on solar power.

Brain coral looks like a giant human brain made of stone. Some brain corals can live for over 500 years!

These corals are extremely strong and heavy, so can survive cyclones and huge waves crashing over them.

To make a safe place to live, some animals drill or use acid to melt burrows into brain coral.

ANCIENT GIANTS
BRAIN CORAL
(Platygyra species*)*

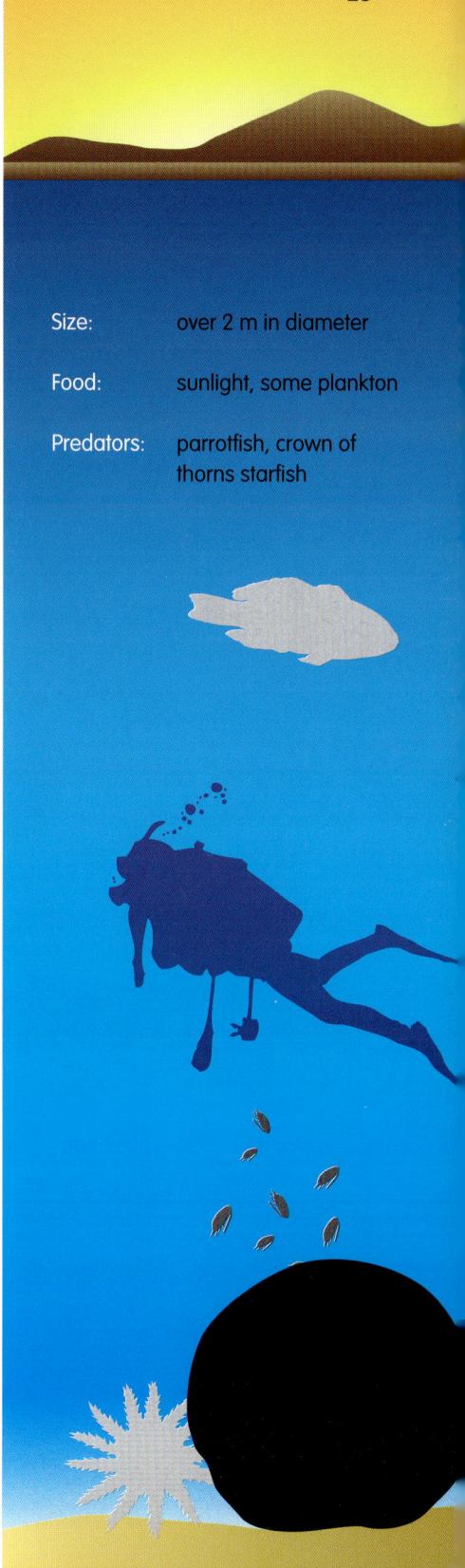

Size:	over 2 m in diameter
Food:	sunlight, some plankton
Predators:	parrotfish, crown of thorns starfish

FLYING GIANTS
MANTA RAY
(Manta birostris)

Manta rays are not dangerous like their cousins the stingrays, as they have no sting in their tail.

Manta rays are the size of a table-tennis table, and can weigh over 2000 kilograms! They fly through the water using their 'wings', and have flaps on the sides of their mouths to help them steer schools of **plankton** and fish into their throats. The plankton is trapped against the ray's net-like gills while the water is squirted out.

When corals release their eggs all at the same time, manta rays come in and feast on the eggy soup.

Size: 7 m across

Food: plankton, small fish

Predators: sharks

TREES OF STONE
STAGHORN CORAL
(*Acropora* species)

The most common types of corals on the Great Barrier Reef are the staghorn corals. They are shaped like giant branching trees, and are as strong as stone.

The gaps between their branches mean that big waves can crash over them without breaking the coral.

Lots of other types of coral also make up the Great Barrier Reef, including plate corals, brain corals, mushroom corals and soft corals.

Staghorn coral makes a safe home for millions of small fishes and other animals. If a shark goes by, everybody can duck into the safety of the coral branches.

Size:	4 m
Food:	mainly sunlight, some plankton
Predators:	fish, crown of thorns starfish

CLIMATE CHANGE: WHAT WE CAN DO

Climate change is a big threat to the Great Barrier Reef.

When it gets too warm, the corals have to spit out the little zooxanthellae plant cells that make their food, because the cells make so much oxygen that it starts to **corrode** the inside of the coral. This is called coral bleaching, as it causes the corals to turn white. The corals are still alive but they need cooler water before they can start growing zooxanthellae again. If the water doesn't cool down, the coral will die.

Lots of carbon dioxide in the air is also a problem as it dissolves in the sea and makes it harder for corals to make their skeletons.

We all have to act quickly to protect the Great Barrier Reef. There are many things we can do to fight climate change. Here are some things we can do straight away.

The Great Barrier Reef is one of the largest and richest areas of coral reef on earth, home to thousands of marine species.

- Plant trees and other plants wherever and whenever you can
- Ride, walk or use public transport instead of using a car
- Stop using dish washers—wash your dishes by hand
- Stop using clothes dryers—dry your clothes outside or on racks
- Stop using air conditioners—open up the windows instead
- Get your school to explore things they can do to be more environmentally friendly
- Find out about renewable energy like wind, solar and other sorts of power
- Find ways to help your local wildlife
- Make things last longer, and learn to fix broken things so you don't have to buy lots of stuff—everything uses some sort of energy to manufacture, which contributes to global warming
- Reduce, reuse, recycle

GLOSSARY AND INDEX

Glossary

anemone: a soft-bodied animal with a central mouth and lots of stinging tentacles

atoll: a ring of islands or reefs

cay: a sand bank island that rises above water level

channel: the gap between reefs, like a gutter

climate change: the warming of the planet caused by pollution and many human activities

colony: a group of small similar-looking animals all living together

coral: a type of sea creature consisting of many small animals working together to make the skeleton on which they live

corrode: to be eaten away or dissolved

invertebrate: types of animals that have no backbone

lagoon: the calm waters inside a ring of reefs

parasite: an animal that lives on or in the bodies of other animals by eating flesh or drinking blood

plankton: tiny creatures that float in the waters of the open ocean

polyp: the tiny living bits of corals that look like small fat trees where the branches are stinging tentacles

predator: an animal that eats other animals

prey: the food of a particular animal

reef face: the strongest corals, which hold back the force of the ocean waves.

solar: from the sun

species: the scientific name for a type of creature, be it animal, plant, bacteria or fungus

symbiosis: when two creatures work together to help each other

Index

anemone 5, 13
animals 3, 7, 13, 23, 27
atoll 7
Blackside Hawkfish 4
Blue-ribbon Eel 17
Brain Coral 23, 27
breathing 16
cay 7
cells 8
channel 7
Cleaner shrimp 10
Cleaner wrasse 10
climate change 3, 28-29
Clown fish 12-13
colours 17
coral 2, 3, 4, 8, 9, 15, 21, 22, 25, 26-27
coral bleaching 28-29
diving 16
divers 16, 19
eggs 21, 25
Emperor Angelfish 4
feeding 13, 15, 19, 21, 24, 25
food 8, 28
Giant clam 22
Glass shrimp 5
Green turtle 20-21
hunting 16, 17, 19
invertebrate 6
jellyfish 4, 21
lagoon 7
Lionfish 11
male/female 13, 17, 21
Manta ray 24-25
nautilus 7
Nudibranch 9
Olive Sea Snake 16
parasite 10
Parrotfish 14-15
plankton 24
poison 9, 11
polyp 2, 5,
potato cod 18-19
predator 17
Ring-tailed Maori Wrasse 4
Saddled Butterflyfish 5
size 6
sleep 14, 21,
slime 13, 19
smell 16
solar power 3-4, 9, 13, 22, 28-29
species 6
Staghorn coral 26-27
sunlight 2-3, 8, 9, 22
swimming 16, 21
symbiosis 13
teeth 15, 17
tentacles 13, 21
venom 16
zooxanthellae 8, 9, 13, 22, 28

Websites:

ReefEd:

www.reefed.edu.au

Australian Marine Conservation Society:

www.amcs.org.au

Great Barrier Reef Marine Park Authority:

www.gbrmpa.gov.au

Australian Conservation Foundation:

www.acfonline.org.au